The
SMALL and MIGHTY
Book of
Planet Earth

Published in 2022 by OH!.
An imprint of Welbeck Children's Limited, part of Welbeck Publishing Group.
Based in London and Sydney.

www.welbeckpublishing.com

Writer: Catherine Brereton
Illustrator: Kirsti Davidson
Design and text by Raspberry Books Ltd
Editorial Manager: Joff Brown
Design Manager: Matt Drew
Production: Melanie Robertson

ISBN 978 1 83935 150 1

Printed in Heshan, China

10 9 8 7 6 5 4 3 2 1

FSC
www.fsc.org
MIX
Paper from
responsible sources
FSC® C020056

The
SMALL and MIGHTY
Book of
Planet Earth

Catherine Brereton and Kirsti Davidson

Contents

Land and Sea
75

Life on Earth
101

People on our
Planet
127

INTRODUCTION

This little book is absolutely
bursting with facts
about Planet Earth.

Planet Earth is our home.
It is a huge rocky ball in space.
Around two-thirds of it is covered
in water. The most special
thing about Earth is that
it supports life.

On Earth
you will find . . .

🍃 rocks from space

🍃 a volcano that stopped
airplane traffic

🍃 a city where sharks once
swam through the streets

🍃 a bird that flies
from one end of the
Earth to the other and
back every year

. . . and lots more.

8

The
Earth
in
Space

EARTH

IS ONE OF EIGHT PLANETS THAT TRAVEL
AROUND OUR STAR, THE SUN. MERCURY,
VENUS, EARTH, AND MARS ARE HUGE BALLS
OF METAL AND ROCK. JUPITER, SATURN,
URANUS, AND NEPTUNE ARE ENORMOUS
BALLS MADE MAINLY OF GAS. THE SUN
AND ALL THE PLANETS, MOONS, AND OTHER
SPACE OBJECTS THAT TRAVEL AROUND IT
ARE CALLED THE SOLAR SYSTEM.

PLANET EARTH

is 4.54 billion years old!

EARTH MEASURES ROUGHLY 24,900 MI. AROUND ITS MIDDLE AND IT HAS A SURFACE AREA OF 200 MILLION SQUARE MI.

IT IS NOT PERFECTLY ROUND LIKE A BALL BUT **BULGES OUT** VERY SLIGHTLY AROUND ITS MIDDLE.

13

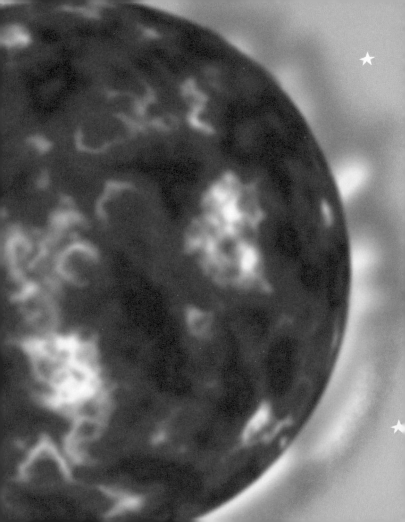

THE EARTH ORBITS (OR TRAVELS
ALL THE WAY ROUND) THE SUN ONCE EVERY
A 365-AND-A-QUARTER DAYS (ROUGHLY).
THIS IS AN EARTH YEAR.

Sunlight takes
about 8 MINUTES
AND 20 SECONDS
to reach Earth.

Because
365-and-a-quarter
is not a whole number, we have
an extra day—A LEAP DAY—
usually every four years to keep
our calendar in time
with Earth's orbit.

15

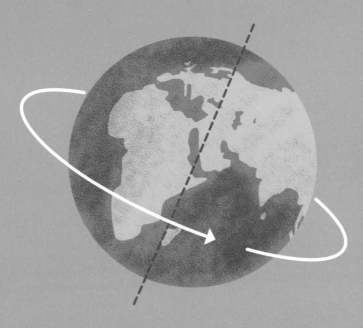

At the same time as traveling around
the Sun, the Earth spins around and
around. It takes **24 HOURS**.
This is one day and night.

The Earth spins really fast—around
1,029 MPH at the equator. But we don't
feel it spinning, as we are moving smoothly
along with it, and because the speed
doesn't change at all.

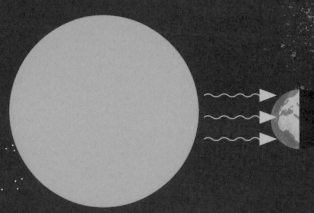

As it spins, some parts of
the Earth are facing the Sun.
It's **DAYTIME** there. Other parts
are facing away from the Sun
and it's **NIGHTTIME** there.

When dinosaurs lived on Earth,

the planet was spinning faster!
Over 65 million years ago, a day on
Earth was shorter and it spun around more
times in a year. The pull of the Moon is
very gradually slowing Earth's spin.

The ancient Greeks called
Earth Gaia, which means
"mother goddess."

All life needs **water**. Water stays liquid
on Earth because Earth is just the right distance
from the Sun – not too hot and not too cold.
It is sometimes called "the **Goldilocks planet**,"
after Goldilocks' porridge in the fairy tale.

Atmosphere

The Earth is covered
by a blanket of air called
THE ATMOSPHERE. This helps
protect it from the full strength of the
Sun's rays. Air contains gases including
oxygen, which all animals need
to breathe.

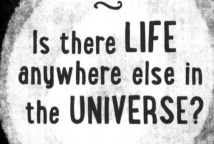

Is there LIFE anywhere else in the UNIVERSE?

As far as we know, **Earth** is the only place where life exists. Scientists have found evidence that there was liquid water on the surface of Mars long ago, so perhaps there was life. They are looking for the **building blocks of life** on Europa, one of Jupiter's moons, or Titan, one of Saturn's moons.

The top and bottom ends of the Earth are called the **North Pole** and **South Pole**. Around the middle of the Earth is an imaginary line called the

EQUATOR.

The half of the Earth above the line is the **northern hemisphere** and the half below it is the **southern hemisphere**.

northern hemisphere

When it is **SUMMER** in the northern hemisphere, the days are longer and the nights are shorter.

equator

At the same time, it is **WINTER** in the southern hemisphere, with shorter days and longer nights.

southern hemisphere

Inside Earth

The surface of
the **EARTH**
is a rocky crust up
to **37 MI.** thick.

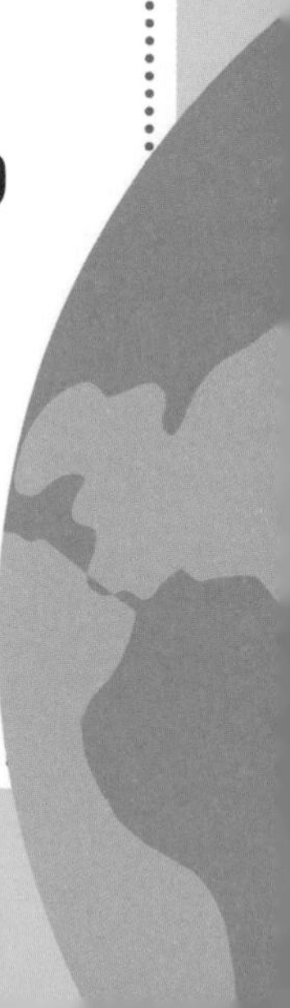

In many places the rock is obvious for us to see, whereas elsewhere the rock is beneath soil and vegetation or under the ocean.

crust

Underneath the crust is the **mantle** –
a layer of extremely hot, solid rock.
Underneath that is a molten **outer core**
and then a solid **metal inner core**.
Right at the center it is unbelievably
hot – it's around 9,750°F, which is
about as hot as the Sun's surface.

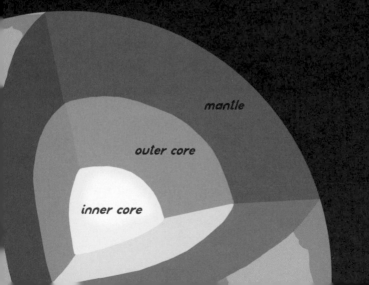

mantle

outer core

inner core

THE EARTH'S CORE is made mainly of IRON, LIKE A BIG MAGNET.

The Earth as a whole is approximately one-third iron, a bit less than a third oxygen, plus large amounts of silicon and magnesium and small amounts of many other substances.

The three main groups of ROCKS on Earth:

MOST IGNEOUS ROCKS ARE FORMED WHEN LAVA (EXTREMELY HOT, FIERY, MELTED ROCK) SPILLS OUT OF THE EARTH'S CRUST AND COOLS DOWN.

SEDIMENTARY ROCKS ARE FORMED WHEN TINY PIECES OF OTHER ROCK, OR TINY PIECES OF SEA CREATURES, SAND AND MUD, SETTLE ON TOP OF EACH OTHER UNDERWATER. OVER MILLIONS OF YEARS THEY GET SQUASHED TOGETHER INTO LAYERS OF ROCK.

METAMORPHIC ROCKS ARE ROCKS THAT STARTED OFF AS OTHER TYPES OF ROCKS AND HAVE BEEN CHANGED BY GREAT HEAT AND OFTEN GREAT PRESSURE.

34

ROCKS FORM INTO AMAZING SHAPES.

Limestone forms spectacular underground caves. They contain pillar-like columns sticking up from the ground, called stalagmites, and spikes like icicles hanging from the ceiling, called stalactites.

Remember: stalacTITES stick TIGHT to the ceiling; stalagMITES MIGHT grow up to meet them.

SOME ROCKS COME FROM SPACE!

They are called meteorites, which are chunks of space rock or metal that fall to Earth. The Hoba meteorite in Namibia is the largest ever found. It is around 60 tonnes —that's about as heavy as 10 elephants!

Rocks are made up of minerals. These can be tiny grains or crystals that fit together in regular patterns.

GEMSTONES are rare minerals that can be cut and polished into jewels. Gems for every color of the rainbow (and more) include . . .

RED	ruby, garnet, red jasper, carnelian
ORANGE	orange citrine, orange topaz
YELLOW	yellow citrine, yellow topaz, yellow diamond
GREEN	emerald, green beryl, jade
BLUE	blue sapphire, aquamarine, turquoise, lapiz lazuli
PURPLE	amethyst
PINK	rose quartz, peach sapphire, pink diamond
WHITE	white diamond
BLACK	black onyx, jet

There are about **1,900** active **VOLCANOES** on Earth.

A volcano is a gap in the Earth's crust where hot gases and melted rock from deep inside the Earth burst out of the surface.

Hot melted rock underneath the Earth's surface is known as **MAGMA.** When it bursts above the surface in a volcanic eruption it is known as **LAVA.**

41

In 2010, a volcano in Iceland with the tricky name of

EYJAFJALLAJÓKULL

(say "AY-a-fyat-la-YEU-koot-la") erupted and sent a cloud of ash over 5 mi. into the sky.

For six days, the ash cloud made it too dangerous for airplanes to fly anywhere in a huge area of the northern hemisphere.

THE EARTH'S CRUST IS BROKEN UP INTO
ENORMOUS PIECES CALLED **TECTONIC
PLATES,** WHICH FLOAT ON THE MELTED
ROCK UNDERNEATH. THE PLATES RUB
TOGETHER AND SOMETIMES SUDDENLY
SHIFT AND CAUSE AN **EARTHQUAKE.**
THIS IS WHEN THE EARTH SHAKES
AND HUGE CRACKS CAN APPEAR.

THERE ARE MILLIONS OF EARTHQUAKES
EVERY YEAR! AROUND 17 OF THEM ARE
CLASSED AS MAJOR EARTHQUAKES.
CHINA, INDONESIA, IRAN, TURKEY, AND
JAPAN HAVE THE MOST EARTHQUAKES.

THE BEST BUILDINGS ARE DESIGNED
SO THAT IN AN EARTHQUAKE THEY
SWAY INSTEAD OF **COLLAPSING.**
IN TURKEY THERE IS A WHOLE
AIRPORT THAT DOES THIS.

THREE SURPRISING
facts about
EARTHQUAKES:

The city of San Francisco, California, is moving towards Los Angeles at a rate of 2 in. a year because each city is on a different tectonic plate.

In 2015, an earthquake caused the world's highest mountain, Mount Everest, to shrink by 1 in. It has got bigger again since.

Many animals can sense the small shifts and vibrations that lead up to an earthquake and will move away to safety. Before a devastating earthquake in 2004, elephants in Sri Lanka ran for higher ground.

47

FOSSILS
are traces of long-dead plants and animals that you can see in rocks.

The fossils formed long ago when those plant or animal remains changed to rocks that have the same shapes.

Ammonites look like spiral-shelled snails, but they are the remains of sea creatures, relatives of squid and octopus, that lived between 419 and 66 million years ago.

The ammonite's shell has **lots of spaces or sections**. When it was alive, the animal kept growing new, larger sections and kept moving its body into the newest, biggest one.

FOSSIL FUELS,

such as coal and oil, are
made of the fossil traces of
prehistoric plants and animals
that have been crushed together for millions
of years. We drill or mine under the Earth to
get at them. Burning fossil fuels provides a lot
of energy, but they pollute the air and
cause the world to warm up.

SOME GREEN SOURCES OF ENERGY (NO FOSSIL FUELS HERE!)

1. Wind power—wind turbines
2. Water power—dams, water wheels, turbines at sea
3. Solar power—solar panels
4. Geothermal power—in some places the heat from magma underground can be used to heat water and drive generators to make electricity

solar panels

Water
and
Weather

Earth is sometimes called
"THE BLUE PLANET"
because of how watery it is.
Water covers around two-thirds
of its surface.

~

APOLLO 17 ASTRONAUTS TOOK A FAMOUS **PHOTO OF EARTH** FROM SPACE IN 1972. THEY SHOWED THAT IT LOOKS LIKE A **PRECIOUS BLUE MARBLE** IN SPACE.

Nearly all of
Earth's water is
SALTY WATER
in the oceans
and seas.

56

OCEANS ARE HUGE AREAS OF SALTY WATER AND THERE ARE FIVE OF THEM:

1. Atlantic Ocean
2. Pacific Ocean
3. Arctic Ocean
4. Indian Ocean
5. Southern Ocean

Seas are smaller areas—but still pretty big!—such as the Mediterranean Sea, the Caribbean Sea, and the North Sea.

ONLY A SMALL AMOUNT
OF EARTH'S WATER IS
FRESH WATER.
AND LESS THAN A QUARTER OF
THAT IS FRESH WATER IN RIVERS,
STREAMS AND FRESHWATER LAKES.
THE REST IS LOCKED UP IN
GLACIERS AND POLAR ICE,
FLOATING IN THE ATMOSPHERE OR
IN SOIL UNDERGROUND.

Some of the water floating in the atmosphere is in the form of a gas called water vapor.

WE ARE WATERY, TOO!
AROUND THREE-FIFTHS
OF AN ADULT HUMAN'S
BODY IS WATER.

Water, air, and the Sun
together make the

WEATHER.

The Sun's energy makes air
warm up and starts the movement
of air all around the planet.
Warm air rises and cooler air
rushes to take its place.

This moving air is the wind—rising, sinking, blowing, and swirling. Wind blows clouds across the sky.

Wind makes the ocean move, too. A gentle wind makes little waves and a strong wind makes high, powerful, sometimes dangerous waves.

All the time, air is moving in giant sweeps around our planet. Jet streams are huge bands of wind that blow over long distances high in the atmosphere. They carry storms and other weather with them.

THREE FIERCE FACTS ABOUT WILD WINDS:

1. TROPICAL STORMS ARE SUPER-STRONG, WITH WIND SPEEDS OF MORE THAN 74 MPH.

2. THEY CAN BE CALLED HURRICANES, CYCLONES, OR TYPHOONS, DEPENDING ON WHERE IN THE WORLD THEY HAPPEN.

3. US AIR FORCE HURRICANE HUNTERS FLY PLANES RIGHT INTO THE HEART OF A HURRICANE, SO THEY CAN FIND OUT WHERE IT IS GOING AND HOW FAST.

Water moves around between
the Earth's surface and the
atmosphere in a never-ending
circle called **THE WATER CYCLE.**

2. Plants give off water vapor too,
and this mixes into the air.

1. Water on the surface (rivers,
lakes, and oceans) is heated up
by the Sun and evaporates,
or turns into water vapor.
It mixes into the air.

3. High up in the sky where the air is cool. water vapor cools and turns into droplets of liquid water. These bunch together and form clouds.

4. Clouds get bigger and the water droplets get heavier until they fall from the sky as rain. hail, sleet, or snow.

5. Water flows into streams and rivers or soaks through the ground and ends up in rivers. lakes. and oceans again.

You might be drinking the same water that was once swallowed by a dinosaur! The water in the water cycle is the same water that has been moving around for **4 BILLION YEARS!**

In a rainforest, it can take
a single raindrop **TEN MINUTES**
to trickle its way from the highest
treetops down to the forest floor.

A DROP OF RAIN spends about
10 days drifting along in
a cloud before falling
down to Earth.

The rainiest place in the world is Mawsynram, Meghalaya, India. It gets **467 IN.** of rain every year on average.

It once rained so much
in Ipswich, Australia, that the
city was flooded and **SHARKS**
swam through the streets!

It's not just the wind that makes ocean water move. There are tides, too. They happen when the Moon and Sun pull on the Earth.

At the seaside, the tide goes in and out twice every day. When it goes in, water gets deeper and covers much of the beach. When it goes out, the water gets shallower and the beach reappears.

At the Bay of Fundy in Nova Scotia,
Canada, the water is 53.5 ft. deeper
at high tide than it is at low tide,
on average. These are the highest
tides in the world.

PLASTIC POLLUTION

is a huge problem in the world's oceans. The plastic we throw away ends up flowing into rivers and then into the ocean. It poisons, traps, and chokes wildlife.

THE
GREAT PACIFIC
GARBAGE PATCH

IS MADE UP OF TWO ENORMOUS
AREAS OF FLOATING PLASTIC
RUBBISH AND PLASTIC SLUDGE
THAT HAVE COLLECTED WHERE
THE CURRENT HAS TAKEN THEM.

74

Land
and
Sea

~ The ~
# EARTH'S
surface has seven
ENORMOUS
pieces of land called
CONTINENTS.
They are:

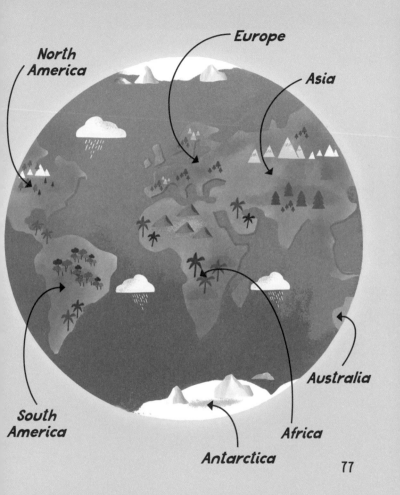

North America

Europe

Asia

South America

Antarctica

Africa

Australia

77

The continents were once all
JOINED TOGETHER.
ABOUT 250 MILLION YEARS AGO THEY MADE
UP A SUPERCONTINENT CALLED PANGAEA.
OVER MILLIONS OF YEARS THE EARTH'S TECTONIC
PLATES DRIFTED APART AND SPLIT UP INTO
THE SEVEN CONTINENTS WE KNOW TODAY.

Pangaea

PLANET EARTH'S

land takes a variety of
different shapes. There are
high mountains, deep
valleys, and flat land.

Some mountains are formed
where the Earth's tectonic plates
have crashed together
and pushed up giant
peaks of rock.

This takes millions of years.

Other mountains are formed by
volcanic eruptions. Lava bursts
through a gap in the Earth's crust
and cools in a dome shape
around the gap.

The world's 10 HIGHEST MOUNTAINS are all in the Himalayas, a vast mountain range stretching through parts of India, Pakistan, Afghanistan, China, Bhutan, and Nepal.

Mount Everest

THE HIGHEST MOUNTAINS ON EACH CONTINENT ARE:

〜

ASIA: Mount Everest 29,035 ft.
SOUTH AMERICA: Mount Aconcagua 22,831 ft.
AFRICA: Kilimanjaro 19,340 ft.
EUROPE: Mount Elbrus 18,356 ft.
NORTH AMERICA: Denali 18,000 ft.
ANTARCTICA: Vinson Massif, 16,050 ft.
AUSTRALIA: Mawson Peak, 9,006 ft.

There are
UNDERWATER
mountains too.

ONE UNDERWATER MOUNTAIN IS EVEN
TALLER THAN MOUNT EVEREST. THE TOP OF

MAUNA KEA

IN HAWAII, UNITED STATES, IS
13,803.5 FT. ABOVE SEA LEVEL BUT
STRETCHES AROUND 19,685 FT. UNDER
THE SEA, MAKING IT MORE THAN
32,800 FT. TALL OVERALL.

MOUNTAINS

are dramatic, wild places. Many mountain tops are covered in snow year-round, and it may be too cold for trees to grow there.

As you go higher and higher the air starts to get thinner, which means there is less oxygen for animals or people to breathe.

IN THE ANDES MOUNTAINS IN
SOUTH AMERICA, LLAMAS HAVE
THICK FUR TO KEEP WARM AND
THEIR BLOOD IS SPECIALLY
ADAPTED SO THEY CAN GET
ENOUGH OXYGEN EVEN THOUGH
THE AIR IS THIN.

The land is shaped by being worn down by water, wind, or huge rivers of ice called glaciers. This wearing down is called

EROSION.

The Grand Canyon, a spectacular valley in the United States, was formed as the Colorado River cut a path through layers of rock. Durdle Door in Dorset, UK, is a natural arch formed by the sea eroding the soft limestone cliffs.

89

SOIL

is a very important feature of the land.

It is like a skin on the surface of the rock. It is made up of pieces of rock, dead plants and animals rotting away, hundreds of living things such as fungi, bacteria, and little animals such as earthworms, as well as water and air.

Soil allows plants to grow. It holds their roots, stores goodness, helps filter and clean water, and helps stop flooding. Healthy soil is vital to the health of the planet.

One tablespoon of soil can be home to up to **40 BILLION** living things!

91

COASTS

are the places where land meets the sea.

SOME LANDFORMS TO LOOK OUT FOR AROUND THE COAST:

Cliff

Stack

Island

Arch

THE WORLD'S TEN LARGEST ISLANDS ARE:

1. Greenland (Denmark)

2. New Guinea (Papua New Guinea and Indonesia)

3. Borneo (Indonesia, Malaysia and Brunei)

4. Madagascar (Madagascar)

5. Baffin Island (Canada)

6. Sumatra (Indonesia)

7. Honshu (Japan)

8. Victoria Island (Canada)

9. Great Britain (UK)

10. Ellesmere Island (Canada)

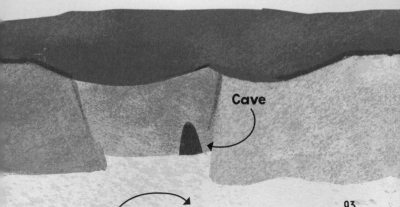

Cave

Beach

93

How deep is the OCEAN?

THE DEEPEST PLACE
ON EARTH IS THE

MARIANA TRENCH,

A BIG DITCH IN THE PACIFIC OCEAN.
IT'S 36,200 FT. DEEP. THAT'S SO DEEP
THAT IT COULD SWALLOW UP 34 EIFFEL
TOWERS ON TOP OF EACH OTHER!

THE BOTTOM OF THE DEEP OCEAN
IS MORE MYSTERIOUS THAN THE
SURFACE OF THE MOON AND FEWER
PEOPLE HAVE BEEN THERE.
HARDLY ANY OF IT HAS EVEN
BEEN EXPLORED YET.

95

The Earth's surface is a very varied place with its deep oceans, high peaks, rivers, deserts, glaciers, and plains. Another thing that varies around the globe is climate.

Climate is the pattern
of weather in a part of
the world, not just from
one day to another but
over many years. One
of the main things that
affects climate is how far
somewhere is from the
equator. The height and
shape of the land and
the oceans also have
an effect.

Today, the world's

CLIMATE IS CHANGING.

Human actions are making it happen.
Burning fossil fuels puts more carbon
dioxide and other "greenhouse gases"
into the atmosphere so that it traps
more of the Sun's heat and the
world warms up.

This worldwide rise in temperature is
called global warming. It is bad news.
It means ice at the poles is melting and
sea levels are rising. It warms the seas,
so plankton and other creatures die.

It causes problems in
many habitats and makes
life difficult for living things.
It leads to storms, droughts, and
floods happening more often.

Life
on
Earth

sequoia tree

There are around **NINE BILLION**
different kinds of living things on
Earth—from the huge **BLUE WHALE**
and towering giant **SEQUOIA TREE**
to tiny animals, plants, and
bacteria too small to see.

~

There has been life
on Earth for around

3.4 BILLION YEARS!

The first living things were
bacteria. Simple plants first
appeared around 500 million
years ago and humans have been
alive for around 2.5 million years.

GROUPS OF LIVING THINGS:

1. Animals
2. Plants
3. Fungi
4. Everything else – including bacteria, algae (such as seaweed), and many microscopic living things.

plants

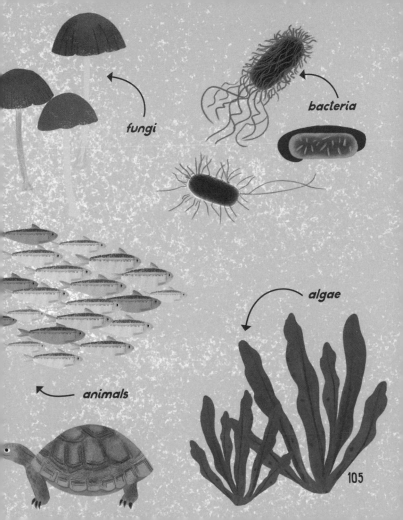

fungi

bacteria

algae

animals

105

The type of place where something lives is called its

HABITAT.

The right habitat has everything a living thing needs to survive.

Galapagos pink iguana

SOME LIVING THINGS CAN ONLY
SURVIVE IN A VERY PARTICULAR HABITAT.
THE **GALAPAGOS PINK IGUANA** ONLY
LIVES ON ONE VOLCANO IN THE GALAPAGOS ISLANDS.

Others can live across large areas
of the planet and in a variety of
habitats. The **RED FOX** lives
in forest, grassland, desert,
mountain, farmland, and even
city habitats in many parts
of the world.

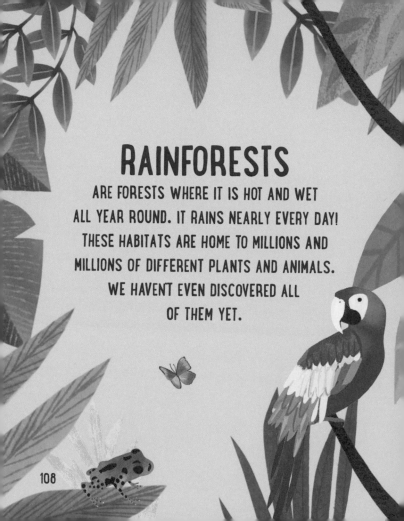

RAINFORESTS

ARE FORESTS WHERE IT IS HOT AND WET
ALL YEAR ROUND. IT RAINS NEARLY EVERY DAY!
THESE HABITATS ARE HOME TO MILLIONS AND
MILLIONS OF DIFFERENT PLANTS AND ANIMALS.
WE HAVENT EVEN DISCOVERED ALL
OF THEM YET.

The Amazon rainforest has 400 BILLION TREES!

Four-fifths of the flowers in AUSTRALIAN rainforests are not found anywhere else in the world.

THE SAVANNA

is a type of grassland in Africa.
The grass provides plenty of food
for large numbers of big animals
including antelopes, giraffes,
zebras, and buffaloes. They roam
from place to place looking for fresh
juicy grass and green leaves to
eat. Then animals such as lions,
leopards and crocodiles, chase
and hunt them to eat.

ELEPHANTS

and other giant savanna animals
need huge spaces to roam free, find
food, and live their lives. Sadly, their
habitat is being destroyed. Farming,
towns, and roads are cutting into
their space and the desert
is growing.

HOT DESERTS

are very dry places. They have little vegetation and are usually very hot during the day and very cold at night. They are difficult habitats for animals and plants to live in.

The fennec fox lives in the desert. It comes out at night when it is cooler, and its hearing is sharp enough to find a tiny beetle crawling along the sand several feet away. Its huge ears aren't just for hearing—heat escapes through them and keeps the fox cool.

113

POLAR HABITATS

ARE SOME OF THE MOST EXTREME ON EARTH. TEMPERATURES DROP AS LOW AS -58°F IN WINTER. WINTER DAYS ARE JUST A FEW HOURS LONG.

orca

The **Arctic** is the area around the North Pole. It is made up of the Arctic Ocean and the lands around it.

The **Antarctic** is the area around the South Pole. It is made up of the continent of Antarctica and the ocean around it.

The cold polar seas are full of life. As well as whales, seals, orcas, and penguins there are FISH and PLANKTON. Plankton are tiny animals and plants too small to see, which are food for bigger animals.

~
ARCTIC WILDLIFE

INCLUDES WALRUS, HARP
SEALS, BELUGA WHALES,
POLAR BEARS, MUSK OXEN,
AND REINDEER. THEY ALL HAVE
CLEVER WAYS TO COPE WITH
THE COLD. REINDEER HAVE
AMAZING NOSES THAT WARM
THE AIR THEY BREATHE
IN, SO THAT IT'S NOT TOO
COLD WHEN IT GETS TO
THE REINDEER'S LUNGS.

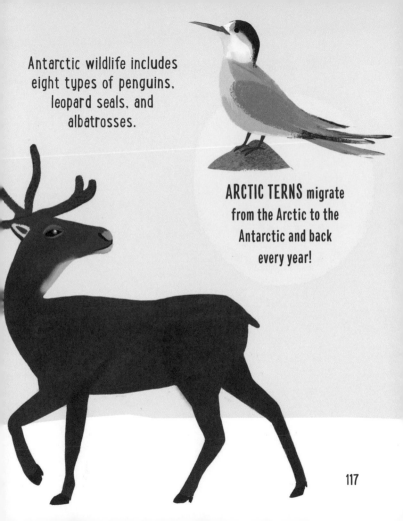

Antarctic wildlife includes eight types of penguins, leopard seals, and albatrosses.

ARCTIC TERNS migrate from the Arctic to the Antarctic and back every year!

117

~ OCEANS ~
are the world's
BIGGEST HABITAT.

They are home to around
20,000 SPECIES
of fish!

THERE ARE MANY DIFFERENT HABITATS IN THE OCEANS.
CORAL REEFS ARE LIKE COLORFUL UNDERWATER
FORESTS SHELTERING A HUGE VARIETY OF ANIMALS.
THE **DEEP OCEAN** IS DARK AND COLD. IT IS HOME
TO SOME VERY STRANGE-LOOKING CREATURES SUCH AS
THE ANGLERFISH, WHICH **GLOWS IN THE DARK!**

PLANTS

have the amazing ability to

MAKE FOOD

from # SUNLIGHT.

This is called photosynthesis.
Their leaves are like little factories.
They take in carbon dioxide from
the air and water from the rain and
the soil, and use the Sun's energy
to turn these into sugars, which
they store up in their bodies, and
oxygen, which they release
into the air.

All animals depend on plants.
They breathe in the OXYGEN that
plants have made, and they
eat plants (or eat other animals
that in turn eat plants).
So life depends on other life.

Many plants depend on animals in return. Most plants with flowers need

INSECTS

to pollinate them so that they can make seeds and grow new plants.

SIX STAR POLLINATORS:

∿

1. Bees
2. Ants
3. Hoverflies
4. Butterflies
5. Moths
6. Beetles

∿

~ PLANTS ~

take in carbon dioxide and give off oxygen, which is important for keeping the atmosphere in balance. They also help keep the land cool—think how cool it is when you are sitting under the shade of a large, leafy tree compared to out in the open sunshine.

MORE THAN HALF OF THE
OXYGEN
MADE ON EARTH IS MADE
BY PLANT PLANKTON IN THE
OCEANS. AROUND A THIRD
IS PRODUCED BY

TROPICAL
RAINFORESTS.

~

People
on our
Planet

There are more than
7.8 BILLION
people on Planet Earth.

PEOPLE RELY ON THE EARTH FOR
EVERYTHING WE NEED TO LIVE:
FOOD TO EAT, WATER TO DRINK,
AIR TO BREATHE, MATERIALS TO
BUILD WITH. BUT ALL THESE
RESOURCES ARE PRECIOUS AND
WE NEED TO TAKE CARE NOT
TO SPOIL THEM OR USE
THEM ALL UP.

People have arranged
the world into

COUNTRIES.

A country is an area
of land run by a single
government.

There are 195 countries
in the world. The biggest is

RUSSIA

which covers about 6.56 million
square mi. The smallest is the
Vatican City at just
0.17 square mi.

The
COUNTRIES
with the
MOST
PEOPLE
are (roughly):

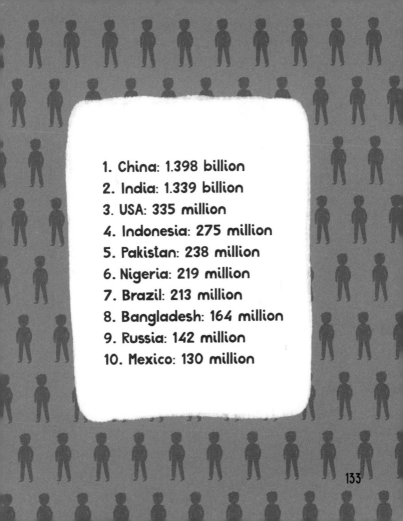

1. China: 1.398 billion
2. India: 1.339 billion
3. USA: 335 million
4. Indonesia: 275 million
5. Pakistan: 238 million
6. Nigeria: 219 million
7. Brazil: 213 million
8. Bangladesh: 164 million
9. Russia: 142 million
10. Mexico: 130 million

People live in all sorts and sizes of settlements, from remote farms or small villages to towns and cities where thousands or

MILLIONS

of people live close together. More than half of the world's people live in cities.

THESE ARE THE CITIES WITH THE MOST PEOPLE:

1. Tokyo, Japan: 37 million
2. Delhi, India: 29 million
3. Shanghai, China: 26 million
4. Sao Paulo, Brazil: 22 million
5. Mexico City, Mexico: 21 million

THE WORLD'S NEWEST COUNTRY IS
SOUTH SUDAN,
WHICH BECAME INDEPENDENT IN 2011.
THE OLDEST IS—YOU MIGHT BE
ABLE TO GUESS—EGYPT.

Only one country in the whole world is named
after a real-life woman. It is the small
island country of

ST. LUCIA

in the Caribbean, which was named after St. Lucia
of Syracuse. According to legend, French sailors
were shipwrecked on the island on St. Lucia's
day, so they named the island after her.

There are around 25 countries named after
individual men. They include Bolivia, named
after the political leader Simón Bolivar, China,
named after China's first emperor Qin, and
the Philippines, after King Philip II of Spain.

People have made some
amazing things on the planet.
Over 4,000 years ago
people worked out how
to transport rocks more than
155 mi and built

STONEHENGE.

People have built spectacular
palaces, cathedrals, temples,
bridges, and skyscrapers.

139

People have worked out how to
SURVIVE
all over the world, to grow
crops to eat, raise animals for
food, and harness energy
to power transport, factories,
and our homes.

PEOPLE NEED TO DO ALL THESE
THINGS, BUT OFTEN WE ARE DOING THEM
IN A WAY THAT IS **NOT SUSTAINABLE**.
THIS MEANS WE ARE USING UP THE WORLD'S
RICHES, AND NOT REPLACING THEM. WE NEED
TO FIND WAYS TO LIVE WITHOUT
DOING SO MUCH **DAMAGE**
TO THE EARTH.

FIVE

things we can do to look after our precious

EARTH:

1.
USE LESS ENERGY AND USE CLEANER ENERGY

2.
BUY LESS, CUT THE PLASTIC, AND REDUCE, REUSE, AND RECYCLE

3.
EAT LESS MEAT

4.
PLANT A TREE

5.
MAKE A HOME FOR POLLINATORS

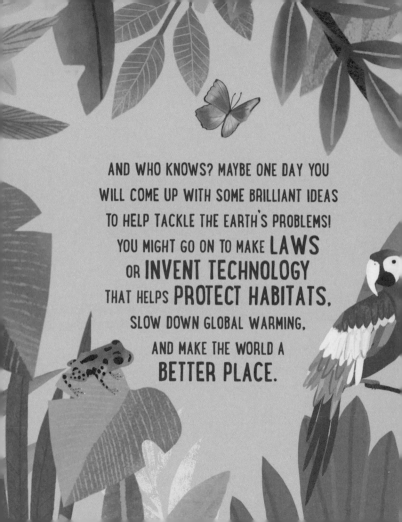

AND WHO KNOWS? MAYBE ONE DAY YOU WILL COME UP WITH SOME BRILLIANT IDEAS TO HELP TACKLE THE EARTH'S PROBLEMS! YOU MIGHT GO ON TO MAKE **LAWS** OR **INVENT TECHNOLOGY** THAT HELPS **PROTECT HABITATS**, SLOW DOWN GLOBAL WARMING, AND MAKE THE WORLD A **BETTER PLACE.**